Big Rocks, Small Rocks

Adria F. Klein

DOMINIE PRESS
Pearson Learning Group

ISBN 0-7685-1508-4

Printed in Singapore

11 12 13 V0ZF 14 13 12 11 10

Dominie
Press
Pearson Learning Group

1-800-321-3106
www.pearsonlearning.com

Table of Contents

Big rocks, small rocks,
make a hill.

Big rocks, small rocks,
make a house.

Big rocks, small rocks,
make a wall.

Big rocks, small rocks,
make a road.

Big rocks, small rocks,
make a tunnel.

Big rocks, small rocks,
make a slope.

Big rocks, small rocks,
make many things.

Picture Glossary

house:

tunnel:

road:

wall:

Index